Mysql interview questions and answers

What's MySQL ?

MySQL (pronounced "my ess cue el") is an open source relational database management system (RDBMS) that uses Structured Query Language (SQL), the most popular language for adding, accessing, and processing data in a database. Because it is open source, anyone can download MySQL and tailor it to their needs in accordance with the general public license. MySQL is noted mainly for its speed, reliability, and flexibility.

...

What Is mSQL?

Mini SQL (mSQL) is a light weight relational database management system capable of providing rapid access to your data with very little overhead. mSQL is developed by Hughes Technologies Pty Ltd.

MySQL was started from mSQL and shared the same API.

Mysql interview questions and answers

What Is SQL?

SQL, SEQUEL (Structured English Query Language), is a language for RDBMS (Relational Database Management Systems). SQL was developed by IBM Corporation.

What is DDL, DML and DCL ?

If you look at the large variety of SQL commands, they can be divided into three large subgroups. Data Definition Language deals with database schemas and descriptions of how the data should reside in the database, therefore language statements like CREATE TABLE or ALTER TABLE belong to DDL. DML deals with data manipulation, and therefore includes most common SQL statements such SELECT, INSERT, etc. Data Control Language includes commands such as GRANT, and mostly concerns with rights, permissions and other controls of the database system.

Mysql interview questions and answers

How do you get the number of rows affected by query?
SELECT COUNT (user_id) FROM users would only return the number of user_id's.

If the value in the column is repeatable, how do you find out the unique values?
Use DISTINCT in the query, such as SELECT DISTINCT user_firstname FROM users; You can also ask for a number of distinct values by saying SELECT COUNT (DISTINCT user_firstname) FROM users;

How do you return the a hundred books starting from 25th?
SELECT book_title FROM books LIMIT 25, 100. The first number in LIMIT is the offset, the second is the number.

You wrote a search engine that should retrieve 10 results at a time, but at the same time you'd like to know how many rows there're total. How do you display that to the user?
SELECT SQL_CALC_FOUND_ROWS page_title FROM web_pages LIMIT 1,10; SELECT FOUND_ROWS(); The second query (not that COUNT() is never used) will tell you how many results there're total, so you can display a phrase "Found

13,450,600 results, displaying 1-10". Note that FOUND_ROWS does not pay attention to the LIMITs you specified and always returns the total number of rows affected by query.

Explain about MySQL and its features.

MySQL is a relational database management system which is an open source database.

Features:

- Because of its unique storage engine architecture MySQL performance is very high.
- Supports large number of embedded applications which makes MySql very flexible.
- Use of Triggers, Stored procedures and views which allows the developer to give a higher productivity.
- Allows transactions to be rolled back, commit and crash recovery.

Mysql interview questions and answers

What are the disadvantages of MySQL?

Answer

- MySQL does not support a very large database size as efficiently
- MySQL does not support ROLE, COMMIT, and Stored procedures in versions less than 5.0
- Transactions are not handled very efficiently.

What are the security recommendations while using MySQL?

Answer

- Access to the user table should never be given to avoid SQL injection attacks.
- Privileges such as GRANT and REVOKE must be made use of.
- SHOW GRANTS can be used to see the list of users who have access
- Never run the MySQL server as the Unix root user

Mysql interview questions and answers

What are MyISAM tables?

Answer
In MySQL MyISAM is the default storage engine. MyISAM tables store data values with the low byte first. Even though MyISAM tables are very reliable, corrupted tables can be expected if there is a hardware failure, the pc shuts down unexpectedly. MyISAM tables are reliable because any change made to a table is written before the sql statement returns. Even though MyISAM is the default storage engine it is advisable to specify ENGINE= MYISAM

What are MyISAM tables?

Answer
In MySQL MyISAM is the default storage engine. MyISAM tables store data values with the low byte first. Even though MyISAM tables are very reliable, corrupted tables can be expected if there is a hardware failure, the pc shuts down unexpectedly. MyISAM tables are reliable because any change made to a table is written before the sql statement returns. Even

though MyISAM is the default storage engine it is advisable to specify ENGINE= MYISAM

Explain the difference between MyISAM Static and MyISAM Dynamic.

MyISAM Static tables have fields of fixed width while the MyISAM Dynamic can accommodate variable lengths such as TEXT, BLOB etc. MyISAM allows easier restoration of data as compared to MyISAM dynamic.

What does myisamchk do?

Myisamchk gets is used to fetch information about the database tables. It is also used to check, repair and optimize the tables. From shell, Myisamchk can be invoked by typing:

Shell> myisamchk [options] tbl_name.
Here options explains what is expected from the Myisamchk.

Mysql interview questions and answers

Explain advantages of InnoDB over MyISAM.

- InnoDb supports locking of rows while MyISAM supports only table locking.
- Data integrity is more in InnoDB.
- Transactional nature of InnoDB enables easy and online backups.

Explain advantages of MyISAM over InnoDB.

- Data is not cached by the MySQL query browser.
- MyISAM is a simple storage engine.
- MyISAM provides more optimization.
- MyISAM has a low relative memory use.

How to use myisamchk to check or repair MyISAM tables?

Myisamchk gets is used to fetch information about the database tables. It is also used to check, repair and optimize the tables. From shell, Myisamchk can be invoked by typing:

Shell> myisamchk [options] tbl_name.

Here options explains what is expected from the Myisamchk.

How to Check MyISAM Tables for Errors?

Using the –myisamchk table_name command can be used to find all errors. it cannot find corruption that involves only the data file. The different options are:

Myisamchk –m table_name – checks index entries for errors and calculates checksum. This checksum that is calculated for all key values of rows is verified with the keys in the index tree.

Myisamchk –e table_name – performs and extended check. does a complete and thorough check of all data

Explain the options of myisamchk to improve the performance of a table.

Myisamchk has a couple of options to optimize a table.

- Using myisamchk –r table_name, runs myisamchk in recovery mode. This option combines the fragmented rows and gets rid of wasted space.
- --Analyze, -a is used for analyze the distribution of key values.
- --sort-index, -S – Sorts index tree.
- --sort-records=index_num, -R index_num – sorts recods according to particularr index.

Discuss about MyISAM Key Cache.

MyISAM keeps a key cache to minimize disk I/O. it keeps the most frequently accessed table blocks in memory. For most frequently accessed index blocks, key cache is used. The key cache is not used for data blocks. Multiple threads can access the cache concurrently. The size of the key cache is restricted using key_buffer_size system variable. If the value of this variable is 0, no key cache is used.

Discuss about MyISAM Index Statistics Collection.

MyISAM's Index statistics collection is based on a set of rows with the same key prefix value. Here, these set of rows are called as value group. The statistics about the tables is used by the optimizer. The average value of the group size plays an improtant role. The group size is used estimate how many rows must be read for each ref access and how many rows will a particular join will produce. Myisam_stats_method system variable if set as global, affects statistics collection for all tables.

What is HEAP table?

Answer
Tables that are present in the memory are called as HEAP tables. When creating a HEAP table in MySql, user needs to specify the TYPE as HEAP. These tables are now more commonly known as memory tables. These memory tables never have values with data type like "BLOB" or "TEXT". They use indexes which make them faster.

What is Query Cache in MySQL?

Answer

Query Cache in MySQL is used in scenarios when the same queries need to be executed on the same data set. These queries also return the same result. Query cache is most useful when there are tables that are not expected to change very often. It is important to note that the query cache does not return old data. If the tables are modified, any important entries in the query cache are flushed.

How is Exception Handling handled in MySQL?

Answer

Exception handling means changing the usual expected flow of the code. This needs to be done to avoid errors. The exceptions in MySql can be handled using the following syntax:

DECLARE handler_type (Continue | Exit) HANDLER FOR condition_value[,...] sp_statement

Here, whenever an error occurs, the handler type value will decide whether to continue or Exit. Continue will execute the next Sql statement while exit will exit the procedure. Condition_value can take number of levels of categories. set condition is used to define code to be performed if the handler is called.

What are the Performance and Scalability characteristics of MySQL?

Answer
MySQL has a unique storage engine architecture that makes it adaptable to most servers. MySQL meets the expectations of the most common applications, i.e. to run millions of transactions. Features like strong memory cache, indexing etc adds to the performance.

MySQL being open source allows customization which allows users to add their own requirements. MySQL also supports large number of embedded applications. These features add to the scalability characteristic.

Mysql interview questions and answers

What are the limitations of mysql in Comparison of Oracle?

Answer

- Transactions are better supported in Oracle as compared to Mysql. ROLE feature is available in Oracle and not in MySQL in versions less than 5.0
- Large Database size is supported more in Oracle in contrast to MySql.

MySQL vs. Oracle.

- Unlike oracle, mysql data types can store invalid dates and don't support time zones.
- Transactions are better supported in Oracle as compared to Mysql. ROLE feature is available in Oracle and not in MySQL in versions less than 5.0
- Large Database size is supported more in Oracle in contrast to MySql.
- Replication in oracle is two way while one way in mysql.

What is a Trigger in MySQL? Define different types of Trigger

Answer

A trigger is a set of code which is executed in response to some event.

E.g Update employee_perfomance table when a new task is inserted in task table. Here, the trigger is "update" and the event is "inserting a new row".

A trigger in MySQL is created using CREATE TRIGGER trigger_name. we need to specify the trigger type.

- When do you want the trigger to execute? This can be either BEFORE or AFTER
- What do you expect the trigger to do? This can be INSERT UPDATE DELETE
- On which table you want the trigger to run? (using ON table_name)
- Lastly, though not mandatory, is FOR EACH ROW if it is used then the trigger will fire once for all records of

the table. If it is not specified the trigger will fire once only regardless of the number of records being updated

What is the difference between CHAR_LENGTH and LENGTH in MySQL?

CHAR_LENGTH, as the name suggests, returns the number of characters / character count. The LENGTH returns the number of bytes / bytes count. To count the Latin characters, both lengths are the same. To count Unicode and other encodings, the lengths are different.

Explain the difference between BOOL, TINYINT and BIT in MySQL.

BOOL: Used to store Boolean values, 0 being false and 1 being true. MySQL sets them as TINYINT type.
TINYINT: The range of this data type is -128 - +127 or 0 – 256 and occupies 1 byte.
BIT: Bit uses 8 bytes and stores only binary data.

What are ENUMs used for in MySQL?

ENUM is used to limit the values that persist in the table. The following example illustrates the best use of ENUM.
CREATE TABLE months (month ENUM 'January', 'February', 'March',);
INSERT months VALUES ('April');

Explain MySQL Aggregate Functions.

Answer
Aggregate functions in MySQL are a group of functions that are used to operate on a set of values. These functions ignore NULL values unless specified. Functions like AVG(), MIN(), MAX(), COUNT() etc fall under this category. As they operate on a set of values, if no Group by clause is used, it applies to all rows.

Explain the following functions with an example.

AVG()
Returns the average of the parameter passed. Returns 0 if no matching rows found.

Example:
Avg(salary)

COUNT()
Counts the number of NON NULL values of the parameter passed. Returns 0 if no matching rows found.

Example:
Select employee_id, COUNT(*) from table_name;

MAX()
Returns the maximum value of the parameter passed. Returns 0 if no matching rows found.

Example:
Select MAX(employee_salary) from table_name

MIN()
Returns the minimun value of the parameter passed. Returns 0 if no matching rows found.

Example:
Select MIN(employee_salary) from table_name

SUM()
Returns the sum of the parameter passed. Returns NULL if no matching rows found.

Example:
Select SUM(employee_salary) from table_name

Describe Transaction-Safe Table Types in MySQL

Answer
While using transactions in MySQL a transaction –safe table type must be used. MyISAM is the default table type. Other transaction-safe table types are InnoDB and BerkeleyDB. MyISAM is much faster and uses less disk space comparatively. However using BDB or InnoDB are much safer in scenarios like hardware failure or pc shut down.

Mysql interview questions and answers

Describe MySQL Connection using mysql binary.

Answer

Establishing connection to MySQL database using Mysql binary can be done at command prompt.

Mysql –u user_name –p

On entering the user name and password the mysql command prompt will be opened to execute any sql statement.

Explain advantages of MyISAM over InnoDB

The following are the advantages of MyISAM over InnoDB:

- MyISAM tables are stored in separate files in compressed mode, where as InnoDB tables are stored in table space.
- More options for further optimization in MyISAM, where as there is no further optimization possible with InnoDB.
- Data except for TEXT and BLOB can occupy at most 8000 bytes in InnoDB.

- Full text indexing available in MyISAM, where as no full text indexing is available for InnoDB.
- Count(*) function's execution is slower in InnoDB because of table space complexity.

MySQL - Stored Procedures and Triggers

Stored Procedures:
A set of SQL statements is called a stored procedure, which can be compiled and stored in the server. The purpose of stored procedures is that, reissuing the entire queries is avoided. The query is parsed only once, thus provides better performance and information passed between server and the client is very less.

Triggers:
A trigger is fired when a particular event occurs. It is also a stored procedure. A stored procedure can be installed which triggers automatically every time a record is deleted or updated or inserted.

Primary Keys and Auto Increment Fields in MySQL

Primary key is used to uniquely identify a row in a table. Usually the primary key is an integer value that could be an auto incremented value. The primary key column can also be a combination of two columns.

The column that is identified for PRIMARY key is defined in the schema as:

PRIMARY KEY (employee_id)

When a column is set to "Auto Increment", its value is automatically incremented in a sequence when a new row is inserted.

COMMIT and ROLLBACK in MySQL

A transaction in MySQL is a set of SQL statements written to perform a specific task. When the transaction is COMMIT, the changes made are saved permanently. ROLLBACK cancels all changes and reverts back the transaction to its state before COMMIT.

It is necessary to commit work in case of system crash

ALTER command to add and drop INDEX in MySQL

An index in MySQL can be added using ALTER statement in multiple ways as shown:

ALTER TABLE tbl_name ADD PRIMARY KEY (column_list)
ALTER TABLE tbl_name ADD UNIQUE index_name (columnlist)
ALTER TABLE tbl_name ADD INDEX index_name (column_list)
ALTER TABLE tbl_name ADD FULLTEXT index_name (column_list)
Drop:
ALTER TABLE table_name DROP PRIMARY KEY;
In order to drop an index that is not a primary key, the name of index should be specified.

Describe MySQL Connection using PHP Script.

The function mysql_connect() establishes the connection to MySQL. To establish the connection, the host name, database user and password is needed. The host is usually a localhost. The ip address 127.0.0.1 can also be specified as the host. The priority depends on the demand.

The following code snippet in PHP describes the connection.

```php
<?php
$dbhost = 'localhost';
$dbuser = 'root';
$dbpass = 'password';
$conn = mysql_connect($dbhost, $dbuser, $dbpass);
mysql_select_db($dbname);
?>
```

After establishing the connection, the database needs to be specified. The last statement in the code snippet performs the selection of the database.

How would you write a query to select all teams that won either 2, 4, 6 or 8 games?
SELECT team_name FROM teams WHERE team_won IN (2, 4, 6, 8)

How would you select all the users, whose phone number is null?
SELECT user_name FROM users WHERE ISNULL(user_phonenumber);

What does this query mean: SELECT user_name, user_isp FROM users LEFT JOIN isps USING (user_id) ?
It's equivalent to saying SELECT user_name, user_isp FROM users LEFT JOIN isps WHERE users.user_id=isps.user_id

How do you find out which auto increment was assigned on the last insert?

SELECT LAST_INSERT_ID() will return the last value assigned by the auto_increment function. Note that you don't have to specify the table name.

Mysql interview questions and answers

What does –i-am-a-dummy flag to do when starting MySQL?
Makes the MySQL engine refuse UPDATE and DELETE commands where the WHERE clause is not present.

On executing the DELETE statement I keep getting the error about foreign key constraint failing. What do I do?
What it means is that so of the data that you're trying to delete is still alive in another table. Like if you have a table for universities and a table for students, which contains the ID of the university they go to, running a delete on a university table will fail if the students table still contains people enrolled at that university. Proper way to do it would be to delete the offending data first, and then delete the university in question. Quick way would involve running SET foreign_key_checks=0 before the DELETE command, and setting the parameter back to 1 after the DELETE is done. If your foreign key was formulated with ON DELETE CASCADE, the data in dependent tables will be removed automatically.

When would you use ORDER BY in DELETE statement?
When you're not deleting by row ID. Such as in DELETE FROM techpreparation_com_questions ORDER BY timestamp

LIMIT 1. This will delete the most recently posted question in the table techpreparation_com_questions.

How can you see all indexes defined for a table?
SHOW INDEX FROM techpreparation_questions;

How would you change a column from VARCHAR(10) to VARCHAR(50)?
ALTER TABLE techpreparation_questions CHANGE techpreparation_content techpreparation_CONTENT VARCHAR(50).

How would you delete a column?
ALTER TABLE techpreparation_answers DROP answer_user_id.

How would you change a table to InnoDB?
ALTER TABLE techpreparation_questions ENGINE innodb;

When you create a table, and then run SHOW CREATE TABLE on it, you occasionally get different results than what you typed in. What does MySQL modify in your newly

created tables?
1. VARCHARs with length less than 4 become CHARs
2. CHARs with length more than 3 become VARCHARs.
3. NOT NULL gets added to the columns declared as PRIMARY KEYs
4. Default values such as NULL are specified for each column

How do I find out all databases starting with 'tech' to which I have access to?
SHOW DATABASES LIKE 'tech%';

How do you concatenate strings in MySQL?
CONCAT (string1, string2, string3)

How do you get a portion of a string?
SELECT SUBSTR(title, 1, 10) from techpreparation_questions;

What's the difference between CHAR_LENGTH and LENGTH?
The first is, naturally, the character count. The second is byte count. For the Latin characters the numbers are the same, but they're not the same for Unicode and other encodings.

Mysql interview questions and answers

How do you convert a string to UTF-8?

SELECT (techpreparation_question USING utf8);

What do % and _ mean inside LIKE statement?
% corresponds to 0 or more characters, _ is exactly one character.

What does + mean in REGEXP?
At least one character. Appendix G. Regular Expressions from MySQL manual is worth perusing before the interview.

How do you get the month from a timestamp?
SELECT MONTH(techpreparation_timestamp) from techpreparation_questions;

How do you offload the time/date handling to MySQL?
SELECT DATE_FORMAT(techpreparation_timestamp, '%Y-%m-%d') from techpreparation_questions; A similar TIME_FORMAT function deals with time.

How do you add three minutes to a date?
ADDDATE(techpreparation_publication_date, INTERVAL 3 MINUTE)

What's the difference between Unix timestamps and MySQL timestamps?
Internally Unix timestamps are stored as 32-bit integers, while MySQL timestamps are stored in a similar manner, but represented in readable YYYY-MM-DD HH:MM:SS format.

How do you convert between Unix timestamps and MySQL timestamps?
UNIX_TIMESTAMP converts from MySQL timestamp to Unix timestamp, FROM_UNIXTIME converts from Unix timestamp to MySQL timestamp.

What are ENUMs used for in MySQL?
You can limit the possible values that go into the table. CREATE TABLE months (month ENUM 'January', 'February', 'March',...); INSERT months VALUES ('April');

Mysql interview questions and answers

How are ENUMs and SETs represented internally?
As unique integers representing the powers of two, due to storage optimizations.

How do you start and stop MySQL on Windows?
net start MySQL, net stop MySQL

How do you start MySQL on Linux?
/etc/init.d/mysql start

Explain the difference between mysql and mysqli interfaces in PHP?
mysqli is the object-oriented version of mysql library functions.

What's the default port for MySQL Server?
3306

What does tee command do in MySQL?
tee followed by a filename turns on MySQL logging to a specified file. It can be stopped by command note.

Mysql interview questions and answers

Can you save your connection settings to a conf file?
Yes, and name it ~/.my.conf. You might want to change the permissions on the file to 600, so that it's not readable by others.

How do you change a password for an existing user via mysqladmin?
mysqladmin -u root -p password "newpassword"

Use mysqldump to create a copy of the database?
mysqldump -h mysqlhost -u username -p mydatabasename > dbdump.sql

Have you ever used MySQL Administrator and MySQL Query Browser?
Describe the tasks you accomplished with these tools.

What are some good ideas regarding user security in MySQL?
There is no user without a password. There is no user without a user name. There is no user whose Host column contains % (which here indicates that the user can log in from anywhere in

the network or the Internet). There are as few users as possible (in the ideal case only root) who have unrestricted access.

Explain the difference between MyISAM Static and MyISAM Dynamic. ?

In MyISAM static all the fields have fixed width. The Dynamic MyISAM table would include fields such as TEXT, BLOB, etc. to accommodate the data types with various lengths. MyISAM Static would be easier to restore in case of corruption, since even though you might lose some data, you know exactly where to look for the beginning of the next record.

What does myisamchk do?
It compressed the MyISAM tables, which reduces their disk usage.

Explain advantages of InnoDB over MyISAM?

Row-level locking, transactions, foreign key constraints and crash recovery.

Explain advantages of MyISAM over InnoDB?

Much more conservative approach to disk space management -

each MyISAM table is stored in a separate file, which could be compressed then with myisamchk if needed. With InnoDB the tables are stored in tablespace, and not much further optimization is possible. All data except for TEXT and BLOB can occupy 8,000 bytes at most. No full text indexing is available for InnoDB. TRhe COUNT(*)s execute slower than in MyISAM due to tablespace complexity.

What are HEAP tables in MySQL?
HEAP tables are in-memory. They are usually used for high-speed temporary storage. No TEXT or BLOB fields are allowed within HEAP tables. You can only use the comparison operators = and <=>. HEAP tables do not support AUTO_INCREMENT. Indexes must be NOT NULL.

How do you control the max size of a HEAP table?
MySQL config variable max_heap_table_size.

What are CSV tables?
Those are the special tables, data for which is saved into comma-separated values files. They cannot be indexed.

Mysql interview questions and answers

Explain federated tables. ?
Introduced in MySQL 5.0, federated tables allow access to the tables located on other databases on other servers.

What is SERIAL data type in MySQL?
BIGINT NOT NULL PRIMARY KEY AUTO_INCREMENT

What happens when the column is set to AUTO INCREMENT and you reach the maximum value for that table?
It stops incrementing. It does not overflow to 0 to prevent data losses, but further inserts are going to produce an error, since the key has been used already.

Explain the difference between BOOL, TINYINT and BIT. ?
Prior to MySQL 5.0.3: those are all synonyms. After MySQL 5.0.3: BIT data type can store 8 bytes of data and should be used for binary data.

Explain the difference between FLOAT, DOUBLE and REAL. ?
FLOATs store floating point numbers with 8 place accuracy and

take up 4 bytes. DOUBLEs store floating point numbers with 16 place accuracy and take up 8 bytes. REAL is a synonym of FLOAT for now.

If you specify the data type as DECIMAL (5,2), what's the range of values that can go in this table?
999.99 to -99.99. Note that with the negative number the minus sign is considered one of the digits.

What happens if a table has one column defined as TIMESTAMP?
That field gets the current timestamp whenever the row gets altered.

But what if you really want to store the timestamp data, such as the publication date of the article?
Create two columns of type TIMESTAMP and use the second one for your real data.

Explain data type TIMESTAMP DEFAULT CURRENT_TIMESTAMP ON UPDATE CURRENT_TIMESTAMP ?

The column exhibits the same behavior as a single timestamp column in a table with no other timestamp columns.

What does TIMESTAMP ON UPDATE CURRENT_TIMESTAMP data type do?

On initialization places a zero in that column, on future updates puts the current value of the timestamp in.

Explain TIMESTAMP DEFAULT '2006:09:02 17:38:44? ON UPDATE CURRENT_TIMESTAMP. ?

A default value is used on initialization, a current timestamp is inserted on update of the row.

If I created a column with data type VARCHAR(3), what would I expect to see in MySQL table?

CHAR(3), since MySQL automatically adjusted the data type

General Information About MySQL
MySQL is a very fast, multi-threaded, multi-user, and robust SQL (Structured Query Language) database server.

Mysql interview questions and answers

MySQL is free software. It is licensed with the GNU GENERAL PUBLIC LICENSE http://www.gnu.org/.

What Is MySQL
MySQL, the most popular Open Source SQL database, is provided by MySQL AB. MySQL AB is a commercial company that builds is business providing services around the MySQL database. See section 1.2 What Is MySQL AB.

ySQL is a database management system.
A database is a structured collection of data. It may be anything from a simple shopping list to a picture gallery or the vast amounts of information in a corporate network. To add, access, and process data stored in a computer database, you need a database management system such as MySQL. Since computers are very good at handling large amounts of data, database management plays a central role in computing, as stand-alone utilities, or as parts of other applications.

MySQL is a relational database management system.
A relational database stores data in separate tables rather than putting all the data in one big storeroom. This adds speed and

flexibility. The tables are linked by defined relations making it possible to combine data from several tables on request. The SQL part of MySQL stands for "Structured Query Language" - the most common standardized language used to access databases.

MySQL is Open Source Software.
Open source means that it is possible for anyone to use and modify. Anybody can download MySQL from the Internet and use it without paying anything. Anybody so inclined can study the source code and change it to fit their needs. MySQL uses the GPL (GNU General Public License) http://www.gnu.org, to define what you may and may not do with the software in different situations. If you feel uncomfortable with the GPL or need to embed MySQL into a commercial application you can buy a commercially licensed version from us.

Why use MySQL?
MySQL is very fast, reliable, and easy to use. If that is what you are looking for, you should give it a try. MySQL also has a very practical set of features developed in very close cooperation with our users. You can find a performance comparison of MySQL to

some other database managers on our benchmark page. See section 12.7 Using Your Own Benchmarks. MySQL was originally developed to handle very large databases much faster than existing solutions and has been successfully used in highly demanding production environments for several years. Though under constant development, MySQL today offers a rich and very useful set of functions. The connectivity, speed, and security make MySQL highly suited for accessing databases on the Internet.

The technical features of MySQL
For advanced technical information, see section 7 MySQL Language Reference. MySQL is a client/server system that consists of a multi-threaded SQL server that supports different backends, several different client programs and libraries, administrative tools, and a programming interface. We also provide MySQL as a multi-threaded library which you can link into your application to get a smaller, faster, easier to manage product. MySQL has a lot of contributed software available.

It is very likely that you will find that your favorite application/language already supports MySQL. The official way to pronounce MySQL is ``My Ess Que Ell" (not MY-SEQUEL). But we try to avoid correcting people who say MY-SEQUEL.

The Main Features of MySQL
The following list describes some of the important characteristics of MySQL:

Fully multi-threaded using kernel threads. That means it can easily use multiple CPUs if available.
C, C++, Eiffel, Java, Perl, PHP, Python and Tcl APIs.
Works on many different platforms.
Many column types: signed/unsigned integers 1, 2, 3, 4, and 8 bytes long, FLOAT, DOUBLE, CHAR, VARCHAR, TEXT, BLOB, DATE, TIME, DATETIME, TIMESTAMP, YEAR, SET, and ENUM types.
Very fast joins using an optimized one-sweep multi-join.
Full operator and function support in the SELECT and WHERE parts of queries. Example:
mysql> SELECT CONCAT(first_name, " ", last_name) FROM tbl_name
WHERE income/dependents > 10000 AND age > 30;

SQL functions are implemented through a highly optimized class library and should be as fast as they can get! Usually there shouldn't be any memory allocation at all after query initialization.

Full support for SQL GROUP BY and ORDER BY clauses.

Support for group functions (COUNT(), COUNT(DISTINCT), AVG(), STD(), SUM(), MAX() and MIN()).

Support for LEFT OUTER JOIN and RIGHT OUTER JOIN with ANSI SQL and ODBC syntax.

You can mix tables from different databases in the same query (as of Version 3.22).

A privilege and password system that is very flexible and secure and allows host-based verification. Passwords are secure because all password traffic is encrypted when you connect to a server.

ODBC (Open-DataBase-Connectivity) support for Win32 (with source). All ODBC 2.5 functions and many others. For example, you can use MS Access to connect to your MySQL server. See section 18 MySQL ODBC Support.

Very fast B-tree disk tables with index compression.

Up to 32 indexes per table are allowed. Each index may consist of 1 to 16 columns or parts of columns. The maximum index length is 500 bytes (this may be changed when compiling

MySQL). An index may use a prefix of a CHAR or VARCHAR field. Fixed-length and variable-length records.

In-memory hash tables which are used as temporary tables.

Handles large databases. We are using MySQL with some databases that contain 50,000,000 records and we know of users that uses MySQL with 60,000 tables and about 5,000,000,000 rows

All columns have default values. You can use INSERT to insert a subset of a table's columns; those columns that are not explicitly given values are set to their default values.

Uses GNU Automake, Autoconf, and libtool for portability.

Written in C and C++. Tested with a broad range of different compilers.

A very fast thread-based memory allocation system.

No memory leaks. Tested with a commercial memory leakage detector (purify).

Includes myisamchk, a very fast utility for table checking, optimization, and repair. See section 15 Maintaining a MySQL Installation.

Full support for several different character sets, including ISO-8859-1 (Latin1), big5, ujis, and more. For example, the Scandinavian characters `@ringaccent{a}', `@"a' and `@"o' are allowed in table and column names.

All data are saved in the chosen character set. All comparisons for normal string columns are case insensitive.

Sorting is done according to the chosen character set (the Swedish way by default). It is possible to change this when the MySQL server is started up. To see an example of very advanced sorting, look at the Czech sorting code. MySQL supports many different character sets that can be specified at compile and run time.

Aliases on tables and columns are allowed as in the SQL92 standard.

DELETE, INSERT, REPLACE, and UPDATE return how many rows were changed (affected). It is possible to return the number of rows matched instead by setting a flag when connecting to the server.

Function names do not clash with table or column names. For example, ABS is a valid column name. The only restriction is that for a function call, no spaces are allowed between the function name and the `(' that follows it. See section 7.39 Is MySQL Picky About Reserved Words?.

All MySQL programs can be invoked with the --help or -? options to obtain online assistance.

Mysql interview questions and answers

The server can provide error messages to clients in many languages. See section 10.1 What Languages Are Supported by MySQL?. Clients may connect to the MySQL server using TCP/IP Sockets, Unix Sockets (Unixes), or Named Pipes (NT). The MySQL-specific SHOW command can be used to retrieve information about databases, tables, and indexes. The EXPLAIN command can be used to determine how the optimizer resolves a query.

Database Basics

Databases are managed by a relational database management system (RDBMS). An RDBMS supports a database language to create and delete databases and to manage and search data. The database language used in almost all DBMSs is SQL, a set of statements that define and manipulate data. After creating a database, the most common SQL statements used are INSERT, UPDATE, DELETE, and SELECT, which add, change, remove, and search data in a database, respectively.

Database

A repository to store data.

Table
The part of a database that stores the data. A table has columns or attributes, and the data stored in rows.

Attributes
The columns in a table. All rows in table entities have the same attributes. For example, a customer table might have the attributes name, address, and city. Each attribute has a data type such as string, integer, or date.

Rows
The data entries in a table. Rows contain values for each attribute. For example, a row in a customer table might contain the values "Matthew Richardson," "Punt Road," and "Richmond." Rows are also known as records.

Relational model
A model that uses tables to store data and manage the relationship between tables.

Relational database management system
A software system that manages data in a database and is based

on the relational model. DBMSs have several components described in detail in Chapter 1.

SQL
A query language that interacts with a DBMS. SQL is a set of statements to manage databases, tables, and data.

Constraints
Restrictions or limitations on tables and attributes. For example, a wine can be produced only by one winery, an order for wine can't exist if it isn't associated with a customer, having a name attribute could be mandatory for a customer.

Primary key
One or more attributes that contain values that uniquely identify each row. For example, a customer table might have the primary key of cust ID. The cust ID attribute is then assigned a unique value for each customer. A primary key is a constraint of most tables.

Index
A data structure used for fast access to rows in a table. An index

is usually built for the primary key of each table and can then be used to quickly find a particular row. Indexes are also defined and built for other attributes when those attributes are frequently used in queries.

Entity-relationship modeling
A technique used to describe the real-world data in terms of entities, attributes, and relationships.

Normalized database
A correctly designed database that is created from an ER model. There are different types or levels of normalization, and a third-normal form database is generally regarded as being an acceptably designed relational database.

MySQL Command Interpreter
The MySQL command interpreter is commonly used to create databases and tables in web database applications and to test queries. Throughout the remainder of this chapter we discuss the SQL statements for managing a database. All these statements can be directly entered into the command interpreter and executed. The statements can also be included in server-side

Mysql interview questions and answers

PHP scripts, as discussed in later chapters.

Once the MySQL DBMS server is running, the command interpreter can be used. The command interpreter can be run using the following command from the shell, assuming you've created a user hugh with a password shhh:

% /usr/local/bin/mysql -uhugh -pshhh The shell prompt is represented here as a percentage character, %.

Running the command interpreter displays the output:

Welcome to the MySQL monitor. Commands end with ; or \g. Your MySQL connection id is 36 to server version: 3.22.38

Type 'help' for help.

mysql>
The command interpreter displays a mysql> prompt and, after executing any command or statement, it redisplays the prompt. For example, you might issue the statement:

mysql> SELECT NOW( );

This statement reports the time and date by producing the following output:

```
+---------------------+
| NOW( ) |
+---------------------+
| 2002-01-01 13:48:07 |
+---------------------+
1 row in set (0.00 sec)
```

mysql>

After running a statement, the interpreter redisplays the mysql> prompt. We discuss the SELECT statement later in this chapter.

As with all other SQL statements, the SELECT statement ends in a semicolon. Almost all SQL command interpreters permit any amount of whitespace—spaces, tabs, or carriage returns—in SQL statements, and they check syntax and execute statements only after encountering a semicolon that is followed by a press of the Enter key. We have used uppercase for the SQL statements throughout this book. However, any mix of upper-

and lowercase is equivalent.

On startup, the command interpreter encourages the use of the help command. Typing help produces a list of commands that are native to the MySQL interpreter and that aren't part of SQL. All non-SQL commands can be entered without the terminating semicolon, but the semicolon can be included without causing an error.

The MySQL command interpreter allows flexible entry of commands and SQL statements:

The up and down arrow keys allow previously entered commands and statements to be browsed and used.

The interpreter has command completion. If you type the first few characters of a string that has previously been entered and press the Tab key, the interpreter automatically completes the command. For example, if wines is typed and the Tab key pressed, the command interpreter outputs winestore, assuming the word winestore has been previously used.

If there's more than one option that begins with the characters entered, or you wish the strings that match the characters to be displayed, press the Tab key twice to show all matches. You can then enter additional characters to remove any ambiguity and press the Tab key again for command completion.

Several common statements and commands are pre-stored, including most of the SQL keywords discussed in this chapter.

To use the default text editor to create SQL statements, enter the command edit in the interpreter. This invokes the editor defined by the EDITOR shell environment variable. When the editor is exited, the MySQL command interpreter reads, parses, and runs the file created in the editor.

When the interpreter is quit and run again later, the history of commands and statements is kept. It is still possible to scroll up using the up arrow and to execute commands and statements that were entered earlier.

You can run commands and SQL statements without actually launching the MySQL command interpreter. For example, to run

SELECT now( ) from the Linux shell, enter the following command:

mysql -ppassword -e "SELECT now( );" This is particularly useful for adding SQL commands to shell or other scripts.

Installing a MySQL Binary Distribution
You need the following tools to install a MySQL binary distribution:
GNU gunzip to uncompress the distribution.
A reasonable tar to unpack the distribution. GNU tar is known to work. Sun tar is known to have problems.
An alternative installation method under Linux is to use RPM (RedHat Package Manager) distributions.

If you run into problems, PLEASE ALWAYS USE mysqlbug when posting questions to mysql@lists.mysql.com. Even if the problem isn't a bug, mysqlbug gathers system information that will help others solve your problem. By not using mysqlbug, you lessen the likelihood of getting a solution to your problem! You will find mysqlbug in the `bin' directory after you unpack the distribution.

Mysql interview questions and answers

The basic commands you must execute to install and use a MySQL binary distribution are:

```
shell> groupadd mysql
shell> useradd -g mysql mysql
shell> cd /usr/local
shell> gunzip < /path/to/mysql-VERSION-OS.tar.gz | tar xvf -
shell> ln -s mysql-VERSION-OS mysql
shell> cd mysql
shell> scripts/mysql_install_db
shell> chown -R mysql /usr/local/mysql
shell> chgrp -R mysql /usr/local/mysql
shell> bin/safe_mysqld --user=mysql &
```

You can add new users using the bin/mysql_setpermission script if you install the DBI and Msql-Mysql-modules Perl modules. A more detailed description follows.

Pick the directory under which you want to unpack the distribution, and move into it. In the example below, we unpack

Mysql interview questions and answers

the distribution under `/usr/local' and create a directory `/usr/local/mysql' into which MySQL is installed. (The following instructions therefore assume you have permission to create files in `/usr/local'. If that directory is protected, you will need to perform the installation as root.)

How to Get MySQL. MySQL binary distributions are provided as compressed tar archives and have names like `mysql-VERSION-OS.tar.gz', where VERSION is a number (for example, 3.21.15), and OS indicates the type of operating system for which the distribution is intended (for example, pc-linux-gnu-i586). Add a user and group for mysqld to run as:
shell> groupadd mysql
shell> useradd -g mysql mysql

These commands add the mysql group and the mysql user. The syntax for useradd and groupadd may differ slightly on different Unixes. They may also be called adduser and addgroup. You may wish to call the user and group something else instead of mysql.
Change into the intended installation directory:
shell> cd /usr/local>

Unpack the distribution and create the installation directory:
shell> gunzip < /path/to/mysql-VERSION-OS.tar.gz | tar xvf -
shell> ln -s mysql-VERSION-OS mysql

The first command creates a directory named `mysql-VERSION-OS'. The second command makes a symbolic link to that directory. This lets you refer more easily to the installation directory as `/usr/local/mysql'.
Change into the installation directory:
shell> cd mysql

You will find several files and subdirectories in the mysql directory. The most important for installation purposes are the `bin' and `scripts' subdirectories.
`bin'
This directory contains client programs and the server You should add the full pathname of this directory to your PATH environment variable so that your shell finds the MySQL programs properly.
`scripts'
This directory contains the mysql_install_db script used to initialize the server access permissions.

Mysql interview questions and answers

If you would like to use mysqlaccess and have the MySQL distribution in some nonstandard place, you must change the location where mysqlaccess expects to find the mysql client. Edit the `bin/mysqlaccess' script at approximately line 18. Search for a line that looks like this:

$MYSQL = '/usr/local/bin/mysql'; # path to mysql executable

Change the path to reflect the location where mysql actually is stored on your system. If you do not do this, you will get a Broken pipe error when you run mysqlaccess.
Create the MySQL grant tables (necessary only if you haven't installed MySQL before):
shell> scripts/mysql_install_db

Note that MySQL versions older than Version 3.22.10 started the MySQL server when you run mysql_install_db. This is no longer true! Change ownership of the installation directory to the user that you will run mysqld as:
shell> chown -R mysql /usr/local/mysql
shell> chgrp -R mysql /usr/local/mysql

The first command changes the owner attribute of the files to the mysql user, and the second changes the group attribute to the mysql group.

If you would like MySQL to start automatically when you boot your machine, you can copy support-files/mysql.server to the location where your system has its startup files. More information can be found in the support-files/mysql.server script itself.

After everything has been unpacked and installed, you should initialize and test your distribution.

You can start the MySQL server with the following command:

shell> bin/safe_mysqld --user=mysql &

MySQL - Quick Installation Overview

The basic commands you must execute to install a MySQL source distribution are:

shell> groupadd mysql
shell> useradd -g mysql mysql
shell> gunzip < mysql-VERSION.tar.gz | tar -xvf -
shell> cd mysql-VERSION

Mysql interview questions and answers

```
shell> ./configure --prefix=/usr/local/mysql
shell> make
shell> make install
shell> scripts/mysql_install_db
shell> chown -R mysql /usr/local/mysql
shell> chgrp -R mysql /usr/local/mysql
shell> /usr/local/mysql/bin/safe_mysqld --user=mysql &
```

If you start from a source RPM, then do the following:

```
shell> rpm --rebuild MySQL-VERSION.src.rpm
```

This will make a binary RPM that you can install.

You can add new users using the bin/mysql_setpermission script if you install the DBI and Msql-Mysql-modules Perl modules. A more detailed description follows.

Pick the directory under which you want to unpack the distribution, and move into it.
If you are interested in using Berkeley DB tables with MySQL, you will need to obtain a patched version of the Berkeley DB

source code. Please read the chapter on Berkeley DB tables before proceeding.

MySQL source distributions are provided as compressed tar archives and have names like `mysql-VERSION.tar.gz', where VERSION is a number like 3.23.33.

Add a user and group for mysqld to run as:

shell> groupadd mysql

shell> useradd -g mysql mysql

These commands add the mysql group, and the mysql user. The syntax for useradd and groupadd may differ slightly on different Unixes. They may also be called adduser and addgroup. You may wish to call the user and group something else instead of mysql.

Unpack the distribution into the current directory:

shell> gunzip < /path/to/mysql-VERSION.tar.gz | tar xvf -

This command creates a directory named `mysql-VERSION'. Change into the top-level directory of the unpacked distribution:

shell> cd mysql-VERSION

Note that currently you must configure and build MySQL from

this top-level directory. You can not build it in a different directory.
Configure the release and compile everything:
shell> ./configure --prefix=/usr/local/mysql
shell> make

When you run configure, you might want to specify some options. Run ./configure --help for a list of options. If configure fails, and you are going to send mail to mysql@lists.mysql.com to ask for assistance, please include any lines from `config.log' that you think can help solve the problem. Also include the last couple of lines of output from configure if configure aborts. Post the bug report using the mysqlbug script.
Install everything:
shell> make install

You might need to run this command as root.
Create the MySQL grant tables (necessary only if you haven't installed MySQL before):
shell> scripts/mysql_install_db

Note that MySQL versions older than Version 3.22.10 started the

MySQL server when you run mysql_install_db. This is no longer true!

Change ownership of the installation to the user that you will run mysqld as:

shell> chown -R mysql /usr/local/mysql
shell> chgrp -R mysql /usr/local/mysql

The first command changes the owner attribute of the files to the mysql user, and the second changes the group attribute to the mysql group.

If you would like MySQL to start automatically when you boot your machine, you can copy support-files/mysql.server to the location where your system has its startup files. More information can be found in the support-files/mysql.server script itself.

After everything has been installed, you should initialize and test your distribution:

shell> /usr/local/mysql/bin/safe_mysqld --user=mysql &

If that command fails immediately with mysqld daemon ended

then you can find some information in the file `mysql-data-directory/'hostname'.err'. The likely reason is that you already have another mysqld server running.

MySQL - MySQL Extensions to ANSI SQL92
MySQL includes some extensions that you probably will not find in other SQL databases. Be warned that if you use them, your code will not be portable to other SQL servers. In some cases, you can write code that includes MySQL extensions, but is still portable, by using comments of the form /*! ... */. In this case, MySQL will parse and execute the code within the comment as it would any other MySQL statement, but other SQL servers will ignore the extensions. For example:

SELECT /*! STRAIGHT_JOIN */ col_name FROM table1,table2 WHERE ...

If you add a version number after the '!', the syntax will only be executed if the MySQL version is equal to or newer than the used version number:

CREATE /*!32302 TEMPORARY */ TABLE (a int);

The above means that if you have Version 3.23.02 or newer, then MySQL will use the TEMPORARY keyword.

MySQL extensions are listed below:

The field types MEDIUMINT, SET, ENUM, and the different BLOB and TEXT types.
The field attributes AUTO_INCREMENT, BINARY, NULL, UNSIGNED, and ZEROFILL.
All string comparisons are case insensitive by default, with sort ordering determined by the current character set (ISO-8859-1 Latin1 by default). If you don't like this, you should declare your columns with the BINARY attribute or use the BINARY cast, which causes comparisons to be done according to the ASCII order used on the MySQL server host.
MySQL maps each database to a directory under the MySQL data directory, and tables within a database to filenames in the database directory. This has a few implications:
Database names and table names are case sensitive in MySQL on operating systems that have case-sensitive filenames (like most Unix systems).

Database, table, index, column, or alias names may begin with a digit (but may not consist solely of digits).

You can use standard system commands to backup, rename, move, delete, and copy tables. For example, to rename a table, rename the `.MYD', `.MYI', and `.frm' files to which the table corresponds.

In SQL statements, you can access tables from different databases with the db_name.tbl_name syntax. Some SQL servers provide the same functionality but call this User space. MySQL doesn't support tablespaces as in: create table ralph.my_table...IN my_tablespace.

LIKE is allowed on numeric columns.

Use of INTO OUTFILE and STRAIGHT_JOIN in a SELECT statement.

The SQL_SMALL_RESULT option in a SELECT statement.

EXPLAIN SELECT to get a description on how tables are joined.

Use of index names, indexes on a prefix of a field, and use of INDEX or KEY in a CREATE TABLE statement.

Use of TEMPORARY or IF NOT EXISTS with CREATE TABLE.

Use of COUNT(DISTINCT list) where 'list' is more than one

element.

Use of CHANGE col_name, DROP col_name, or DROP INDEX, IGNORE or RENAME in an ALTER TABLE statement.

Use of RENAME TABLE.

Use of multiple ADD, ALTER, DROP, or CHANGE clauses in an ALTER TABLE statement.

Use of DROP TABLE with the keywords IF EXISTS.

You can drop multiple tables with a single DROP TABLE statement.

The LIMIT clause of the DELETE statement.

The DELAYED clause of the INSERT and REPLACE statements.

The LOW_PRIORITY clause of the INSERT, REPLACE, DELETE, and UPDATE statements.

Use of LOAD DATA INFILE. In many cases, this syntax is compatible with Oracle's LOAD DATA INFILE.

The ANALYZE TABLE, CHECK TABLE, OPTIMIZE TABLE, and REPAIR TABLE statements.

The SHOW statement.

Strings may be enclosed by either `"' or `", not just by `".

Use of the escape `\' character.

Mysql interview questions and answers

The SET OPTION statement.
You don't need to name all selected columns in the GROUP BY part. This gives better performance for some very specific, but quite normal queries.
One can specify ASC and DESC with GROUP BY.
To make it easier for users who come from other SQL environments, MySQL supports aliases for many functions. For example, all string functions support both ANSI SQL syntax and ODBC syntax.
MySQL understands the || and && operators to mean logical OR and AND, as in the C programming language. In MySQL, || and OR are synonyms, as are && and AND. Because of this nice syntax, MySQL doesn't support the ANSI SQL || operator for string concatenation; use CONCAT() instead. Because CONCAT() takes any number of arguments, it's easy to convert use of the || operator to MySQL.
CREATE DATABASE or DROP DATABASE.
The % operator is a synonym for MOD(). That is, N % M is equivalent to MOD(N,M). % is supported for C programmers and for compatibility with PostgreSQL.
The =, <>, <= ,<, >=,>, <<, >>, <=>, AND, OR, or LIKE operators may be used in column comparisons to the left of the

FROM in SELECT statements. For example:
mysql> SELECT col1=1 AND col2=2 FROM tbl_name;

The LAST_INSERT_ID() function.
The REGEXP and NOT REGEXP extended regular expression operators.
CONCAT() or CHAR() with one argument or more than two arguments. (In MySQL, these functions can take any number of arguments.)
The BIT_COUNT(), CASE, ELT(), FROM_DAYS(), FORMAT(), IF(), PASSWORD(), ENCRYPT(), md5(), ENCODE(), DECODE(), PERIOD_ADD(), PERIOD_DIFF(), TO_DAYS(), or WEEKDAY() functions.
Use of TRIM() to trim substrings. ANSI SQL only supports removal of single characters.
The GROUP BY functions STD(), BIT_OR(), and BIT_AND().
Use of REPLACE instead of DELETE + INSERT.
The FLUSH flush_option statement.
The possiblity to set variables in a statement with :=:
SELECT @a:=SUM(total),@b=COUNT(*),@a/@b AS avg

FROM test_table;
SELECT @t1:=(@t2:=1)+@t3:=4,@t1,@t2,@t3;

MySQL - Running MySQL in ANSI Mode
If you start mysqld with the --ansi option, the following behavior of MySQL changes:

|| is string concatenation instead of OR.
You can have any number of spaces between a function name and the `('. This forces all function names to be treated as reserved words.
`"' will be an identifier quote character (like the MySQL ``' quote character) and not a string quote character. REAL will be a synonym for FLOAT instead of a synonym of DOUBLE.
5.3 MySQL Differences Compared to ANSI SQL92
We try to make MySQL follow the ANSI SQL standard and the ODBC SQL standard, but in some cases MySQL does some things differently:

-- is only a comment if followed by a white space.
For VARCHAR columns, trailing spaces are removed when the value is stored.

In some cases, CHAR columns are silently changed to VARCHAR columns.

Privileges for a table are not automatically revoked when you delete a table. You must explicitly issue a REVOKE to revoke privileges for a table.

NULL AND FALSE will evaluate to NULL and not to FALSE. This is because we don't think it's good to have to evaluate a lot of extra conditions in this case.

MySQL - Functionality Missing from MySQL

The following functionality is missing in the current version of MySQL. For a prioritized list indicating when new extensions may be added to MySQL, you should consult the online MySQL TODO list. That is the latest version of the TODO list in this manual.

MySQL - Sub-selects

The following will not yet work in MySQL:

SELECT * FROM table1 WHERE id IN (SELECT id FROM table2);
SELECT * FROM table1 WHERE id NOT IN (SELECT id

FROM table2);
SELECT * FROM table1 WHERE NOT EXISTS (SELECT id FROM table2 where table1.id=table2.id);

However, in many cases you can rewrite the query without a sub-select:

SELECT table1.* FROM table1,table2 WHERE table1.id=table2.id;
SELECT table1.* FROM table1 LEFT JOIN table2 ON table1.id=table2.id where table2.id IS NULL

For more complicated subqueries you can often create temporary tables to hold the subquery. In some cases, however this option will not work. The most frequently encountered of these cases arises with DELETE statements, for which standard SQL does not support joins (except in sub-selects). For this situation there are two options available until subqueries are supported by MySQL.

The first option is to use a procedural programming language (such as Perl or PHP) to submit a SELECT query to obtain the primary keys for the records to be deleted, and then use these values to construct the DELETE statement (DELETE FROM ... WHERE ... IN (key1, key2, ...)).

The second option is to use interactive SQL to contruct a set of DELETE statements automatically, using the MySQL extension CONCAT() (in lieu of the standard || operator). For example:

SELECT CONCAT('DELETE FROM tab1 WHERE pkid = ', tab1.pkid, ';')
FROM tab1, tab2
WHERE tab1.col1 = tab2.col2;

You can place this query in a script file and redirect input from it to the mysql command-line interpreter, piping its output back to a second instance of the interpreter:

prompt> mysql --skip-column-names mydb > myscript.sql | mysql mydb

MySQL only supports INSERT ... SELECT ... and REPLACE ... SELECT ... Independent sub-selects will probably be available in Version 4.0. You can now use the function IN() in other contexts, however.

MySQL - SELECT INTO TABLE

MySQL doesn't yet support the Oracle SQL extension: SELECT ... INTO TABLE .... MySQL supports instead the ANSI SQL syntax INSERT INTO ... SELECT ..., which is basically the same thing.

Alternatively, you can use SELECT INTO OUTFILE... or CREATE TABLE ... SELECT to solve your problem.

MySQL - Transactions

As MySQL does nowadays support transactions, the following discussion is only valid if you are only using the non-transaction-safe table types.

The question is often asked, by the curious and the critical, ``Why is MySQL not a transactional database?'' or ``Why does MySQL not support transactions?''

MySQL has made a conscious decision to support another

paradigm for data integrity, ``atomic operations.'' It is our thinking and experience that atomic operations offer equal or even better integrity with much better performance. We, nonetheless, appreciate and understand the transactional database paradigm and plan, within the next few releases, to introduce transaction-safe tables on a per table basis. We will be giving our users the possibility to decide if they need the speed of atomic operations or if they need to use transactional features in their applications.

How does one use the features of MySQL to maintain rigorous integrity and how do these features compare with the transactional paradigm?

First, in the transactional paradigm, if your applications are written in a way that is dependent on the calling of ``rollback'' instead of ``commit'' in critical situations, then transactions are more convenient. Moreover, transactions ensure that unfinished updates or corrupting activities are not committed to the database; the server is given the opportunity to do an automatic rollback and your database is saved.

MySQL, in almost all cases, allows you to solve for potential problems by including simple checks before updates and by running simple scripts that check the databases for inconsistencies and automatically repair or warn if such occurs. Note that just by using the MySQL log or even adding one extra log, one can normally fix tables perfectly with no data integrity loss.

Moreover, fatal transactional updates can be rewritten to be atomic. In fact,we will go so far as to say that all integrity problems that transactions solve can be done with LOCK TABLES or atomic updates, ensuring that you never will get an automatic abort from the database, which is a common problem with transactional databases.

Not even transactions can prevent all loss if the server goes down. In such cases even a transactional system can lose data. The difference between different systems lies in just how small the time-lap is where they could lose data. No system is 100% secure, only ``secure enough.'' Even Oracle, reputed to be the safest of transactional databases, is reported to sometimes lose data in such situations.

To be safe with MySQL, you only need to have backups and have the update logging turned on. With this you can recover from any situation that you could with any transactional database. It is, of course, always good to have backups, independent of which database you use.

Mysql interview questions and answers

The transactional paradigm has its benefits and its drawbacks. Many users and application developers depend on the ease with which they can code around problems where an abort appears to be, or is necessary, and they may have to do a little more work with MySQL to either think differently or write more. If you are new to the atomic operations paradigm, or more familiar or more comfortable with transactions, do not jump to the conclusion that MySQL has not addressed these issues. Reliability and integrity are foremost in our minds. Recent estimates indicate that there are more than 1,000,000 mysqld servers currently running, many of which are in production environments. We hear very, very seldom from our users that they have lost any data, and in almost all of those cases user error is involved. This is, in our opinion, the best proof of MySQL's stability and reliability.

Lastly, in situations where integrity is of highest importance, MySQL's current features allow for transaction-level or better reliability and integrity. If you lock tables with LOCK TABLES, all updates will stall until any integrity checks are made. If you only obtain a read lock (as opposed to a write lock), then reads and inserts are still allowed to happen. The new inserted records will not be seen by any of the clients that have a READ lock until they release their read locks. With INSERT DELAYED you can queue inserts into a local queue, until the locks are released, without having the client wait for the insert to complete.

``Atomic," in the sense that we mean it, is nothing magical. It only means that you can be sure that while each specific update is running, no other user can interfere with it, and there will never be an automatic rollback (which can happen on transaction based systems if you are not very careful). MySQL also guarantees that there will not be any dirty reads. You can find some example of how to write atomic updates in the commit-rollback section.

We have thought quite a bit about integrity and performance, and we believe that our atomic operations paradigm allows for both high reliability and extremely high performance, on the order of three to five times the speed of the fastest and most optimally tuned of transactional databases. We didn't leave out transactions because they are hard to do. The main reason we went with atomic operations as opposed to transactions is that by doing this we could apply many speed optimizations that would not otherwise have been possible.

Many of our users who have speed foremost in their minds are not at all concerned about transactions. For them transactions are not an issue. For those of our users who are concerned with or have wondered about transactions vis-a-vis MySQL, there is a ``MySQL way" as we have outlined above. For those where safety is more important than speed, we recommend them to use the BDB tables for all their critical data.

One final note: We are currently working on a safe replication schema that we believe to be better than any commercial replication system we know of. This system will work most reliably under the atomic operations, non-transactional, paradigm. Stay tuned.

MySQL - Stored Procedures and Triggers

A stored procedure is a set of SQL commands that can be compiled and stored in the server. Once this has been done, clients don't need to keep reissuing the entire query but can refer to the stored procedure. This provides better performance because the query has to be parsed only once, and less information needs to be sent between the server and the client. You can also raise the conceptual level by having libraries of functions in the server.

A trigger is a stored procedure that is invoked when a particular event occurs. For example, you can install a stored procedure that is triggered each time a record is deleted from a transaction table and that automatically deletes the corresponding customer from a customer table when all his transactions are deleted. The planned update language will be able to handle stored procedures, but without triggers. Triggers usually slow down everything, even queries for which they are not needed.

MySQL - Foreign Keys

Note that foreign keys in SQL are not used to join tables, but are used mostly for checking referential integrity (foreign key constraints). If you want to get results from multiple tables from a SELECT statement, you do this by joining tables:

SELECT * from table1,table2 where table1.id = table2.id;

The FOREIGN KEY syntax in MySQL exists only for compatibility with other SQL vendors' CREATE TABLE commands; it doesn't do anything. The FOREIGN KEY syntax without ON DELETE ... is mostly used for documentation purposes. Some ODBC applications may use this to produce automatic WHERE clauses, but this is usually easy to override. FOREIGN KEY is sometimes used as a constraint check, but this check is unnecessary in practice if rows are inserted into the tables in the right order. MySQL only supports these clauses because some applications require them to exist (regardless of whether or not they work).

In MySQL, you can work around the problem of ON DELETE ... not being implemented by adding the appropriate DELETE statement to an application when you delete records from a table that has a foreign key. In practice this is as quick (in some cases quicker) and much more portable than using foreign keys.

In the near future we will extend the FOREIGN KEY implementation so that at least the information will be saved in the table specification file and may be retrieved by mysqldump and ODBC. At a later stage we will implement the foreign key constraints for application that can't easily be coded to avoid them.

MySQL - Reasons NOT to Use Foreign Keys constraints
There are so many problems with foreign key constraints that we don't know where to start:
Foreign key constraints make life very complicated, because the

foreign key definitions must be stored in a database and implementing them would destroy the whole ``nice approach'' of using files that can be moved, copied, and removed. The speed impact is terrible for INSERT and UPDATE statements, and in this case almost all FOREIGN KEY constraint checks are useless because you usually insert records in the right tables in the right order, anyway. There is also a need to hold locks on many more tables when updating one table, because the side effects can cascade through the entire database. It's MUCH faster to delete records from one table first and subsequently delete them from the other tables.

You can no longer restore a table by doing a full delete from the table and then restoring all records (from a new source or from a backup).

If you use foreign key constraints you can't dump and restore tables unless you do so in a very specific order. It's very easy to do ``allowed'' circular definitions that make the tables impossible to re-create each table with a single create statement, even if the definition works and is usable.

It's very easy to overlook FOREIGN KEY ... ON DELETE rules when one codes an application. It's not unusual that one loses a lot of important information just because a wrong or misused ON

DELETE rule.

The only nice aspect of FOREIGN KEY is that it gives ODBC and some other client programs the ability to see how a table is connected and to use this to show connection diagrams and to help in building applicatons.

MySQL will soon store FOREIGN KEY definitions so that a client can ask for and receive an answer about how the original connection was made. The current `.frm' file format does not have any place for it. At a later stage we will implement the foreign key constraints for application that can't easily be coded to avoid them.

MySQL - `--' as the Start of a Comment
MySQL doesn't support views, but this is on the TODO.

MySQL - Views
Some other SQL databases use `--' to start comments. MySQL has `#' as the start comment character, even if the mysql command-line tool removes all lines that start with `--'. You can also use the C comment style /* this is a comment */ with MySQL.

MySQL Version 3.23.3 and above supports the `--' comment style only if the comment is followed by a space. This is because this degenerate comment style has caused many problems with automatically generated SQL queries that have used something like the following code, where we automatically insert the value of the payment for !payment!:

UPDATE tbl_name SET credit=credit-!payment!

What do you think will happen when the value of payment is negative?

Because 1--1 is legal in SQL, we think it is terrible that `--' means start comment.

In MySQL Version 3.23 you can, however, use: 1-- This is a comment

The following discussion only concerns you if you are running a MySQL version earlier than Version 3.23:

Mysql interview questions and answers

If you have a SQL program in a text file that contains `--' comments you should use:

shell> replace " --" " #" < text-file-with-funny-comments.sql \
| mysql database

instead of the usual:

shell> mysql database < text-file-with-funny-comments.sql

You can also edit the command file ``in place'' to change the `--' comments to `#' comments:

shell> replace " --" " #" -- text-file-with-funny-comments.sql

Change them back with this command:

shell> replace " #" " --" -- text-file-with-funny-comments.sql

MySQL - How to Cope Without COMMIT/ROLLBACK
The following mostly applies only for ISAM, MyISAM, and HEAP tables. If you only use transaction-safe tables (BDB

tables) in an a update, you can do COMMIT and ROLLBACK also with MySQL.

The problem with handling COMMIT-ROLLBACK efficiently with the above table types would require a completely different table layout than MySQL uses today. The table type would also need extra threads that do automatic cleanups on the tables, and the disk usage would be much higher. This would make these table types about 2-4 times slower than they are today.

For the moment, we prefer implementing the SQL server language (something like stored procedures). With this you would very seldom really need COMMIT-ROLLBACK. This would also give much better performance.

Loops that need transactions normally can be coded with the help of LOCK TABLES, and you don't need cursors when you can update records on the fly.

We at TcX had a greater need for a real fast database than a 100% general database. Whenever we find a way to implement these features without any speed loss, we will probably do it. For the moment, there are many more important things to do. Check the TODO for how we prioritize things at the moment. (Customers with higher levels of support can alter this, so things may be reprioritized.)

The current problem is actually ROLLBACK. Without ROLLBACK, you can do any kind of COMMIT action with LOCK TABLES. To support ROLLBACK with the above table types, MySQL would have to be changed to store all old records that were updated and revert everything back to the starting point if ROLLBACK was issued. For simple cases, this isn't that hard to do (the current isamlog could be used for this purpose), but it would be much more difficult to implement ROLLBACK for ALTER/DROP/CREATE TABLE.

To avoid using ROLLBACK, you can use the following strategy:

Use LOCK TABLES ... to lock all the tables you want to access.
Test conditions.
Update if everything is okay.
Use UNLOCK TABLES to release your locks.

This is usually a much faster method than using transactions with possible ROLLBACKs, although not always. The only situation this solution doesn't handle is when someone kills the threads in the middle of an update. In this case, all locks will be released but some of the updates may not have been executed.

You can also use functions to update records in a single

operation. You can get a very efficient application by using the following techniques:

Modify fields relative to their current value.
Update only those fields that actually have changed.
For example, when we are doing updates to some customer information, we update only the customer data that has changed and test only that none of the changed data, or data that depend on the changed data, has changed compared to the original row. The test for changed data is done with the WHERE clause in the UPDATE statement. If the record wasn't updated, we give the client a message: "Some of the data you have changed have been changed by another user". Then we show the old row versus the new row in a window, so the user can decide which version of the customer record he should use.

This gives us something that is similar to column locking but is actually even better, because we only update some of the columns, using values that are relative to their current values. This means that typical UPDATE statements look something like these:

UPDATE tablename SET pay_back=pay_back+'relative change';

UPDATE customer
SET
customer_date='current_date',
address='new address',
phone='new phone',
money_he_owes_us=money_he_owes_us+'new_money'
WHERE
customer_id=id AND address='old address' AND phone='old phone';

As you can see, this is very efficient and works even if another client has changed the values in the pay_back or money_he_owes_us columns.

In many cases, users have wanted ROLLBACK and/or LOCK TABLES for the purpose of managing unique identifiers for some tables. This can be handled much more efficiently by using an AUTO_INCREMENT column and either the SQL function LAST_INSERT_ID() or the C API function mysql_insert_id().

At MySQL AB, we have never had any need for row-level locking because we have always been able to code around it. Some cases really need row locking, but they are very few. If you want row-level locking, you can use a flag column in the table and do something like this:

UPDATE tbl_name SET row_flag=1 WHERE id=ID;

MySQL returns 1 for the number of affected rows if the row was found and row_flag wasn't already 1 in the original row.
You can think of it as MySQL changed the above query to:

UPDATE tbl_name SET row_flag=1 WHERE id=ID and row_flag <> 1;

MySQL - General Security
Anyone using MySQL on a computer connected to the Internet should read this section to avoid the most common security mistakes.

In discussing security, we emphasize the necessity of fully protecting the entire server host (not simply the MySQL server) against all types of applicable attacks: eavesdropping, altering, playback, and denial of service. We do not cover all aspects of availability and fault tolerance here.

MySQL uses Access Control Lists (ACLs) security for all connections, queries, and other operations that a user may attempt to perform. There is also some support for SSL-encrypted connections between MySQL clients and servers. Many of the concepts discussed here are not specific to MySQL at all; the same general ideas apply to almost all applications.

When running MySQL, follow these guidelines whenever possible:

DON'T EVER GIVE ANYONE (EXCEPT THE MySQL ROOT USER) ACCESS TO THE mysql.user TABLE! The encrypted password is the real password in MySQL. If you know this for one user you can easily login as him if you have access to his 'host'.

Learn the MySQL access privilege system. The GRANT and REVOKE commands are used for restricting access to MySQL. Do not grant any more privileges than necessary. Never grant privileges to all hosts. Checklist:

Try mysql -u root. If you are able to connect successfully to the server without being asked for a password, you have problems. Any user (not just root) can connect to your MySQL server with full privileges! Review the MySQL installation instructions, paying particular attention to the item about setting a root password.

Use the command SHOW GRANTS and check to see who has access to what. Remove those privileges that are not necessary using the REVOKE command.

Do not keep any plain-text passwords in your database. When your computer becomes compromised, the intruder can take the full list of passwords and use them. Instead use MD5() or another one-way hashing function.

Do not use passwords from dictionaries. There are special programs to break them. Even passwords like ``xfish98" are very bad. Much better is ``duag98" which contains the same word ``fish" but typed one key to the left on a standard QWERTY keyboard. Another method is to use ``Mhall" which is taken from the first characters of of each word in the sentence ``Mary had a little lamb." This is easy to remember and type, but hard to guess for someone who does not know it.

Mysql interview questions and answers

Invest in a firewall. This protects from at least 50% of all types of exploits in any software. Put MySQL behind the firewall or in a demilitarized zone (DMZ). Checklist:

Try to scan your ports from the Internet using a tool such as nmap. MySQL uses port 3306 by default. This port should be inaccessible from untrusted hosts. Another simple way to check whether or not your MySQL port is open is to type telnet server_host 3306 from some remote machine, where server_host is the hostname of your MySQL server. If you get a connection and some garbage characters, the port is open, and should be closed on your firewall or router, unless you really have a good reason to keep it open. If telnet just hangs, everything is OK, the port is blocked.

Do not trust any data entered by your users. They can try to trick your code by entering special or escaped character sequences in Web forms, URLs, or whatever application you have built. Be sure that your application remains secure if a user enters something like ``; DROP DATABASE mysql;". This is an extreme example, but large security leaks and data loss may occur as a result of hackers using similar techniques, if you do not prepare for them. Also remember to check numeric data. A common mistake is to protect only strings. Sometimes people think that if a database contains only publicly available data that it need not be protected. This is incorrect. At least denial-of-service type attacks can be performed on such databases. The simplest way to protect from this type of attack is to use apostrophes around the numeric constants: SELECT * FROM table WHERE ID='234' instead of SELECT * FROM table WHERE ID=234. MySQL automatically converts this string to a number and strips all non-numeric symbols from it. Checklist: All WWW applications:

Try to enter `'' and `''' in all your Web forms. If you get any kind of MySQL error, investigate the problem right away.

Try to modify any dynamic URLs by adding %22 (`''), %23 (`#'), and %27 (`'') in the URL.

Try to modify datatypes in dynamic URLs from numeric ones to character ones containing characters from previous examples. Your application should be safe against this and similar attacks.

Try to enter characters, spaces, and special symbols instead of numbers in numeric fields. Your application should remove them before passing them to MySQL or your application should generate an error. Passing unchecked values to MySQL is very dangerous!

Check data sizes before passing them to MySQL.

Consider having your application connect to the database using a different user name than the one you use for administrative purposes. Do not give your applications any more access privileges than they need.

Users of PHP:

Check out the addslashes() function.

Users of MySQL C API:

Check out the mysql_escape() API call.

Users of MySQL++:

Check out the escape and quote modifiers for query streams.

Users of Perl DBI:

Check out the quote() method.

Do not transmit plain (unencrypted) data over the Internet. These data are accessible to everyone who has the time and ability to intercept it and use it for their own purposes. Instead, use an encrypted protocol such as SSL or SSH. MySQL supports internal SSL connections as of Version 3.23.9. SSH port-forwarding can be used to create an encrypted (and compressed) tunnel for the communication.

Learn to use the tcpdump and strings utilities. For most cases, you can check whether or not MySQL data streams are unencrypted by issuing a command like the following:

Mysql interview questions and answers

shell> tcpdump -l -i eth0 -w - src or dst port 3306 | strings

(This works under Linux and should work with small modifications under other systems). Warning: If you do not see data this doesn't always actually mean that it is encrypted. If you need high security, you should consult with a security expert

how to do login in mysql with unix shell?

Answer1-By below method if password is pass and user name is root # [mysql dir]/bin/mysql -h hostname -u root -p pass

how you will Create a database on the mysql server with unix

mysql> create database databasename;

how to list or view all databases from the mysql server.

mysql> show databases;

How Switch (select or use) to a database.

mysql> use databasename;

How To see all the tables from a database of mysql server.

mysql> show tables;

How to see table's field formats or description of table .

mysql> describe tablename;

How to delete a database from mysql server.

mysql> drop database databasename;

How we get Sum of column

mysql> SELECT SUM(*) FROM [table name];

How to delete a table

mysql> drop table tablename;

How you will Show all data from a table.

mysql> SELECT * FROM tablename;

How to returns the columns and column information pertaining to the designated table

mysql> show columns from tablename;

How to Show certain selected rows with the value "pcds"

mysql> SELECT * FROM tablename WHERE fieldname = "pcds";

How will Show all records containing the name "riya" AND the phone number '9112543210'

mysql> SELECT * FROM tablename WHERE name = "riya" AND phone_number = '9112543210';

How you will Show all records not containing the name "riya" AND the phone number '9112543210' order by the phone_number field.

mysql> SELECT * FROM tablename WHERE name != "riya" AND phone_number = '9112543210' order by phone_number;

How to Show all records starting with the letters 'riya' AND the phone number '9112543210'

mysql> SELECT * FROM tablename WHERE name like "riya%" AND phone_number = '9112543210';

How to show all records starting with the letters 'riya' AND the phone number '9112543210' limit to records 1 through 5.

mysql> SELECT * FROM tablename WHERE name like "riya%" AND phone_number = '9112543210' limit 1,5;

Use a regular expression to find records. Use "REGEXP BINARY" to force case-sensitivity. This finds any record beginning with r.

mysql> SELECT * FROM tablename WHERE rec RLIKE "^r";

How you will Show unique records.

mysql> SELECT DISTINCT columnname FROM tablename;

how we will Show selected records sorted in an ascending (asc) or descending (desc)

mysql> SELECT col1,col2 FROM tablename ORDER BY col2 DESC;

mysql> SELECT col1,col2 FROM tablename ORDER BY col2 ASC;

how to Return total number of rows.

mysql> SELECT COUNT(*) FROM tablename;

How to Join tables on common columns.

mysql> select lookup.illustrationid, lookup.personid,person.birthday from lookup left join person on lookup.personid=person.personid=statement to join birthday in person table with primary illustration id

How to Creating a new user. Login as root. Switch to the MySQL db. Make the user. Update privs.

mysql -u root -p mysql> use mysql;

mysql> INSERT INTO user (Host,User,Password) VALUES('%','username',PASSWORD('password'));

mysql> flush privileges;

How to Change a users password from unix shell.

[mysql dir]/bin/mysqladmin –

u username -h hostname.blah.org –

p password 'new-password'

How to Change a users password from MySQL prompt. Login as root. Set the password. Update privs.

mysql -u root -p

Mysql interview questions and answers

mysql> SET PASSWORD FOR 'user'@'hostname' = PASSWORD('passwordhere');

mysql> flush privileges;

How to Recover a MySQL root password. Stop the MySQL server process. Start again with no grant tables. Login to MySQL as root. Set new password. Exit MySQL and restart MySQL server.

/etc/init.d/mysql stop

mysqld_safe --skip-grant-tables &

mysql -u root

mysql> use mysql;

```
mysql> update user set password=PASSWORD("newrootpassword") where User='root';

mysql> flush privileges;

mysql> quit

# /etc/init.d/mysql stop

# /etc/init.d/mysql start
```

How to Set a root password if there is on root password.

```
# mysqladmin -u root password newpassword
```

How to Update a root password.

```
# mysqladmin -u root -p oldpassword newpassword
```

Mysql interview questions and answers

How to allow the user "riya" to connect to the server from localhost using the password "passwd". Login as root. Switch to the MySQL db. Give privs. Update privs.

```
# mysql -u root -p
mysql> use mysql;
mysql> grant usage on *.* to riya@localhost identified by 'passwd';
mysql> flush privileges;
```

How to give user privilages for a db. Login as root. Switch to the MySQL db. Grant privs. Update privs.

```
# mysql -u root -p
mysql> use mysql;
mysql> INSERT INTO user (Host,Db,User,Select_priv,Insert_priv,Update_priv,Delete_priv,Create_priv,Drop_priv) VALUES ('%','databasename','username','Y','Y','Y','Y','Y','N');
mysql> flush privileges;
```

    or

mysql> grant all privileges on databasename.* to username@localhost;

mysql> flush privileges;

How To update info already in a table and Delete a row(s) from a table.

mysql> UPDATE [table name] SET Select_priv = 'Y',Insert_priv = Y',Update_priv = 'Y' where [field name] = 'user'; mysql> DELETE from [table name] where [field name] = 'whatever';

How to Update database permissions/privilages.

mysql> flush privileges;

How to Delete a column and Add a new column to database

mysql> alter table [table name] drop column [column name];mysql> alter table [table name] add column [new column name] varchar (20);

Change column name and Make a unique column so we get no dupes.

mysql> alter table [table name] change [old column name] [new column name] varchar (50);mysql> alter table [table name] add unique ([column name]);

How to make a column bigger and Delete unique from table.

mysql> alter table [table name] modify [column name] VARCHAR(3);

mysql> alter table [table name] drop index [colmn name];

How to Load a CSV file into a table

mysql> LOAD DATA INFILE '/tmp/filename.csv' replace INTO TABLE [table name] FIELDS TERMINATED BY ',' LINES TERMINATED BY '\n' (field1,field2,field3);

How to dump all databases for backup. Backup file is sql commands to recreate all db's.

[mysql dir]/bin/mysqldump -u root -ppassword --opt >/tmp/alldatabases.sql

How to dump one database for backup.

[mysql dir]/bin/mysqldump -u username -ppassword --databases databasename >/tmp/databasename.sql

How to dump a table from a database.

[mysql dir]/bin/mysqldump -c -u username -ppassword databasename tablename > /tmp/databasename.tablename.sql

Restore database (or database table) from backup.

[mysql dir]/bin/mysql -u username -ppassword databasename < /tmp/databasename.sql

How to Create Table show Example

mysql> CREATE TABLE [table name] (firstname VARCHAR(20), middleinitial VARCHAR(3), lastname

VARCHAR(35),suffix VARCHAR(3),officeid VARCHAR(10),userid VARCHAR(15),username VARCHAR(8),email VARCHAR(35),phone VARCHAR(25), groups VARCHAR(15),datestamp DATE,timestamp time,pgpemail VARCHAR(255));

How to search second maximum(second highest) salary value(integer)from table employee (field salary)in the manner so that mysql gets less load?

By below query we will get second maximum(second highest) salary value(integer)from table employee (field salary)in the manner so that mysql gets less load?

SELECT DISTINCT(salary) FROM employee order by salary desc limit 1 , 1 ;(This way we will able to find out 3rd highest , 4th highest salary so on just need to change limit condtion like LIMIT 2,1 for 3rd highest and LIMIT 3,1 for 4th some one may finding this way useing below query that taken more time as compare to above query SELECT salary FROM employee where salary < (select max(salary) from employe) order by salary DESC limit 1 ;

Mysql interview questions and answers

Mysql interview questions and answers

Mysql interview questions and answers

Mysql interview questions and answers

Mysql interview questions and answers

Mysql interview questions and answers

Mysql interview questions and answers

Mysql interview questions and answers

Mysql interview questions and answers

www.ingramcontent.com/pod-product-compliance
Lightning Source LLC
Chambersburg PA
CBHW080909170526
45158CB00008B/2050